RAYMOND SMITH

Confessions of a Pray-er To Be Named Later

A Rookie's Guide to Training for Prayer Victory

DISCIPLE
BLUEPRINT
PRESS

First edition

ISBN: 979-8-9985686-5-7

This book was professionally typeset on Reedsy.
Find out more at reedsy.com

Contents

Dedication

Left to right: Owen, Khloe and Maizon

To Maizon, Khloe, and Owen—

I don't think you will ever fully understand what it means to me to sit on my deck and watch you — running across the fields, throwing passes, flipping cartwheels into the wind, carrying dreams in your hearts bigger than the hills around us.

You don't even realize it yet, but every sprint you take, every throw you make, every laugh you share — is a gift God uses to remind me what hope looks like.

I remember the day you stepped into the cool waters of Potato Creek that runs behind my house. The creek flowed around you. The sky bore witness. And Heaven smiled when you rose from those baptism waters — new, clean, chosen. Aunt Wendy was beaming in Heaven.

That moment will always matter more than any game you will ever win. Because long after the cheers fade and the trophies collect dust, your souls will still be running the most important race — **the race of faith.**

I love you more fiercely than I can say.

You have made my life richer, deeper, and brighter in ways I could have never earned or deserved.

As you grow stronger, faster, and braver, never forget that your greatest strength will not be in your hands, or your feet, but in your heart, surrendered to God.
Be athletes.
Be dreamers.
But above all, be warriors — warriors of prayer, warriors of

faith, warriors of light.
   I will always be your biggest fan.
   I will always be cheering you on.

And I will always be on my knees, praying for you to cross every finish line that matters most.

With all the love a heart can hold,

Uncle Raymond

Introduction: My Confession

"Prayer: the only conversation where it's socially acceptable to fall asleep mid-sentence and the other Person still loves you."
— *Troy Roman (You will get to know him later)*

I write about God. I teach about God. I even preach about God.

You'd think that would automatically qualify me for some kind of varsity-level prayer status—maybe not MVP, but at least a solid sixth man off the bench.

But here's the confession:

If I tried out for a Prayer Team... I'd probably be the first one cut. Not because I don't believe in prayer. I do. Not because I don't want to pray. I honestly do. But because when I actually try to pray... well, let's just say things go sideways fast.

I start off strong—maybe even quoting a Psalm or two—and before you know it, I'm mentally rewriting my grocery list, wondering if I fed the dog, and debating whether I can ask God to help get rid of Jerry Jones so the Cowboys have a shot at winning the Super Bowl again. (See ending prayer)

I usually have **several** important things I need to pray about. But once I start, my prayer turns into a cosmic vending machine request list. Push the right buttons, hope I get what I asked for—and maybe throw in a "Thy will be done" to keep it spiritual.

If there's a prayer rookie level—I'm somewhere *below* that. Prayer amateur? Prayer intern? A **pray-er to be named later**? That's more like it.

But here's the thing—I don't want to stay there.

I want to be the kind of person who doesn't just pray *at* God but walks *with* Him. I want to know what it means to *hear* God, not just talk at Him. I want to pray with power, with purpose, with passion.

I want to be a **Prayer Warrior**—maybe even an All-Star. And who knows? If God hands out plaques, maybe someday I'll make the **Pro Prayer Hall of Fame.**

But right now?

Right now, I'm just trying to stop checking my phone in the middle of a sentence that started with, "Dear Heavenly Father..."

So if you're like me—someone who loves Jesus but doesn't quite have prayer figured out—you're not alone.

This book is my playbook.

It's not written from the winner's podium, but from the locker room, the practice field, the bench, and sometimes the parking lot where I'm wondering if I still belong in the game.

We'll start with the spiritual warm-ups—breaking through guilt and learning how to just *show up.* Then we'll run some drills, learn the playbook, and figure out how to pray through distraction, anxiety, silence, and even heartbreak. There will be stories—some awkward, some funny, and some that still make me cry. But all of them are real.

You won't need a theology degree, a prayer closet, or perfect focus. All you need is a willing heart, a little grit, and the courage to say, "I'm not great at this... but I'm here."

Let's lace up. Let's hit the field.

And let's become the prayer warriors we were meant to be.

1

Chapter 1 – Taking the Field

I write. I teach. I preach. I talk about Jesus a lot. You'd think I'd be a prayer machine by now. But if I'm honest? If prayer were tryouts, I might be the first one cut.

It's not that I don't pray. I do. But often my prayers feel more like hurried halftime speeches than deep locker-room strategy. I get distracted. I forget what I was saying mid-sentence. I start strong, then suddenly I'm thinking about dinner, email, or what happened to that one sock in the dryer.

So let's be real: I'm not writing this book because I'm a prayer warrior. I'm writing it because I want to be one.

This is for every person who feels like prayer is hard. For every believer who wants to pray but doesn't know how. For every soul who's ever said, "I know I should pray more..."

This book is for us.

And if prayer were a sport, this chapter is where we start training.

The Childhood Spark

When I was a kid, I watched the Dallas Cowboys every Sunday. It was the late 60s—Don Meredith, Bob Lilly, and the rest of the Doomsday Defense. I wore a Cowboys jersey to bed and begged for a new football every Christmas because I wore the old ones out in the yard.

Back then, football wasn't just a game. It was a calling.

I played with friends in the yard. Then I joined a YMCA league. Eventually, I played in school. I studied the game. I knew the plays. I could tell you when Tom Landry was going to call a draw play, a screen, or send the house on a blitz.

That kind of passion is what I want for prayer.

I've known people like that—men and women whose prayers shook heaven. When I needed prayer, they were the names I wanted on my side. They were the prayer warriors. The spiritual linebackers.

And I want in the game.

But before I can call plays, I need to learn the basics.

Lombardi's Football

After a tough loss, legendary coach Vince Lombardi gathered his players and began the next practice by holding up the ball and saying, "Men, this is a football."

It sounds simple—even ridiculous—but the point was clear: you can't succeed in the game if you forgot or don't know the fundamentals.

So let's start where we need to:

This... is prayer.

It's not a wish list. It's not just a church thing. It's not a backup plan.

Prayer is relationship. Prayer is power. Prayer is the lifeblood of a believer.

When the Game Changes

Before we get too far, I need to tell you something that shaped this journey for me.

There was a moment I didn't see coming. A diagnosis. A life-defining pivot.

"Stage IV Pancreatic Cancer."

Those four words changed everything.

It wasn't my diagnosis. It was my wife's.

And just like that, I was in a game I had never trained for. No practice reps. No warm-ups. Just fear, confusion, and heartbreak.

I knew God. I knew Scripture. I had faith. But in that moment, I didn't know how to pray.

Would I pray for healing? Would I pray for peace? Would I even pray at all? Because when the love of your life is given a death sentence, words fail.

This book is going to tell more of that story. But for now, I want you to know: I've been where you are. I'm still walking that field.

Let's Get in the Game

I don't want to sit on the bench of my own spiritual life.

I want to run the plays. I want to learn the language. I want to go from being a spiritual spectator to a fully trained prayer warrior.

If that's you too, then let's lace up.

Because it's time to take the field.

2

Chapter 2 – Stretching the Soul: Warming Up for Prayer

Athletes don't walk into the arena cold. They stretch. They breathe. They warm up. Whether it's NBA players using towels to stretch their hamstrings or baseball pitchers tossing soft lobs before bringing the heat, everyone knows the same truth:

You don't perform well without warming up.

So why do I rush into prayer like I've just been subbed in off the bench?

I don't stretch. I don't breathe. I just... pray.

And sometimes, it feels like I pull a spiritual hamstring.

This chapter is all about preparing our hearts, minds, and spirits to step into God's presence with focus, freedom, and full attention.

Because prayer isn't just performance. It's presence.

Why Warm Up Matters

In pro sports, warming up prepares the body for exertion. But it also prepares the **mind**. It tells the brain: "It's game time."

Prayer warm-ups work the same way. They quiet distractions. They center our attention. They prepare our hearts to engage fully with God.

And most of us skip it.

My Own Stretching Season

While I love the Dallas Cowboys, I'm also a huge Texas Rangers fan. When they finally won the World Series, I got emotional. My wife laughed at me for crying over baseball. But if you'd been a Rangers fan as long as I have, you'd get it.

I've been to hundreds of games, watched thousands. One poignant moment I remember is the 2015 playoffs against the Blue Jays. Game 5. Seventh inning.

Elvis Andrus—normally a solid shortstop—misplayed a grounder. Then dropped the ball on a sure out. Then came Bautista's go-ahead homer. The game slipped away.

And after the game, Andrus just sat in the dugout.

The cameras stayed on him. Alone. Watching the other team celebrate.

I said to myself, *This moment will define him. He'll either let it break him—or use it to become better.*

And you know what? He came back stronger.

That's what warming up does. It prepares you **before** the moment comes so you don't freeze—or fold—**during** it.

And that's my problem with prayer sometimes.

When I feel close to God, prayer flows easily.

But when I feel like I've failed—or worse, when I've hurt someone else with my failure—I dread praying. I avoid it.

Why? Because I let guilt be my coach.

I think things like:

- "God's disappointed in me."
- "I don't even deserve to pray right now."
- "I should clean myself up first."

Here's the twist: God already knows. The Holy Spirit is already nudging. He's not waiting for perfection. He's waiting for **honesty**.

Warming up reminds me: I don't pray because I'm perfect. I pray because I'm not.

What Scripture Says About Warming Up to God

Let's look at how Scripture helps us prepare to enter God's presence.

James 4:8 (NLT)

"Come close to God, and God will come close to you. Wash your hands, you sinners; purify your hearts, for your loyalty is divided between God and the world."

This verse isn't about earning God's attention—it's about **alignment**. Drawing near is a choice. God doesn't say, "Fix everything and then come." He says, "Come—and as you do, clean your hands and steady your heart."

Hebrews 4:16 (NLT)

"So let us come boldly to the throne of our gracious God. There we will receive his mercy, and we will find grace to help us when we need it most."

I love the word *boldly*. It doesn't say sheepishly. Or fearfully. It says, "Come like you belong here." Because in Christ, you do. Warming up with this verse reminds me: God isn't annoyed by my need—He's ready to meet it.

Romans 8:26 (NLT)

"And the Holy Spirit helps us in our weakness. For example, we don't know what God wants us to pray for. But the Holy Spirit prays for us with groanings that cannot be expressed in words."

Some days, warming up is just admitting, "God, I don't even know where to start." And the Spirit says, "Don't worry. I've got this."

That's the kind of teammate I need.

Prayer Drill #1 – Stretch Before You Speak

Here's your challenge: take 2–3 minutes before you pray to spiritually stretch.

Try this:

1. **Breathe deeply** for 30 seconds.
2. **Thank God** for 3 specific things.
3. **Confess** anything that's on your heart.
4. **Sit in silence** and say, "God, I'm listening."

Then begin your prayer.

This isn't a rule—it's a rhythm. A way to stretch your soul before stepping into conversation with God.

So next time, before you talk... take time to warm up.

Because this isn't just game day.

This is life.

3

Chapter 3 – Drills and Disciplines: Building a Consistent Prayer Life

In sports, nobody becomes great by playing only on game day. Champions are made in practice. Drills. Reps. Sweat. Repeating the basics until they become muscle memory. Prayer is no different. If we want to grow into strong, consistent pray-ers, we must learn the value of showing up—even when we don't feel like it.

That's where the training really begins.

Let me take you back to my teenage years. My best friend Randy joined a junior bowling league and invited me to come along. It was Saturday mornings, and I had those off, so I said sure.

That first season? I bowled a solid 110 average. Not terrible, but certainly not great. I wanted more. I had my eyes set on a 200 average. That was the number the best junior bowlers were hitting, and I wanted to be one of them.

I worked on my game. Switched from a straight ball to a curve. Focused on spare conversions. Next season, I jumped up to 180.

So, I went to my coach and asked, "What do I need to do to hit

200?"

He said, "What you need to do is simple. But doing it? That's the hard part."

He had watched me bowl. I was a right-hander, and I kept leaving the 10 pin. That pesky back-right pin. The hardest for a right-handed bowler with a curve to pick up. And I missed it. A lot.

"If you want to average over 200," he said, "you need to convert that 10 pin nine out of ten times."

Then he did something that changed my game. After league play, we'd go to a lane where he'd manually set only the 10 pin. And for the next hour, every Saturday, I'd practice nothing but that one spare.

Week after week.

Eventually, I nailed it. I became consistent. And my average jumped to 210.

Consistency. Coaching. Repetition.

That's what changed everything.

And it's what will change your prayer life, too.

Prayer isn't just about breakthrough moments—it's about building muscle memory. Daily connection. Showing up even when you feel spiritually off.

Let's be honest. We all love the idea of powerful prayer, but the practice? That's where most of us struggle. And that's why most people never grow beyond spiritual beginners.

But don't worry. You don't need to pray for an hour. You don't even need to start with ten minutes. You just need to start.

Even Jesus had a prayer routine.

Mark 1:35 (NLT)

"Before daybreak the next morning, Jesus got up and went out to an isolated place to pray."

Let me be clear: if **Jesus** needed to get up early and find quiet time to pray, what makes us think we can wing it? I mean, if I skip caffeine and try to function, it gets ugly fast. Jesus didn't skip the essential things. He made time. Before the world around Him woke up, He was already connecting with the Father.

We can't afford to treat prayer like an optional warm-up. If Jesus prioritized it, we should too. And hey, maybe you're not a morning person—God still hears groggy prayers. Just show up.

Luke 5:16 (NLT)

"But Jesus often withdrew to the wilderness for prayer."

Did you catch that? **Often.** Not once in a while. Not when He had nothing else going on. Jesus withdrew. He pulled away from noise, crowds, miracles, ministry—to pray.

That tells me something really important: prayer wasn't filler for Jesus. It was fuel.

You don't stumble into a deep prayer life. You *withdraw.* You make room. And if the Son of God had to do that, you better believe we do too.

Daniel 6:10 (NLT)

"But when Daniel learned that the law had been signed, he went home and knelt down as usual in his upstairs room, with its windows open toward Jerusalem. He prayed three times a day, just as he had always done, giving thanks to his God."

What I love about this verse is that Daniel didn't start praying **because** of a crisis. He was already praying. Consistency didn't just prepare him for hard times—it carried him *through* them.

And get this: the guy was under threat of being thrown into a den of lions. Real lions. I freak out if I think there might be a bee in the car.

Daniel didn't run, panic, or tweet about it. He went home and prayed—*as usual.*

That's who I want to be. Not a crisis-only pray-er. A consistent one.

And that takes discipline.

Another Daily Discipline

Years ago, one of my favorite relatives, Uncle Bud, developed dementia. It changed him. He became confused and, at times, aggressive—a far cry from the kind and gentle man I grew up with.

He always remembered me. Never remembered my sisters. (I told them it's because they were forgettable, and I was unforgettable.)

That season left a mark on me. And a fear: *What if that happens to me?*

So I started reading about ways to keep your mind sharp. One suggestion kept popping up: mental exercises.

So every morning, for the past **15 years**, I've played Solitaire. I have an app on my iPad that gives me five new games a day. And every single day, without fail, I complete all five.

Whether it helps prevent dementia or not, I've learned something powerful: **discipline is built in the doing.**

And I want that kind of discipline in my prayer life.

Prayer Drill #2: The 7-Day Training Plan

Pick one time of day that you can stick with. Morning, lunch, evening—doesn't matter. Just choose it. Set a reminder. And try this plan for the next 7 days:

1. **Gratitude** – "Lord, thank You for _____."
2. **Confession** – "Lord, I am sorry for _____."
3. **Help** – "Lord, I need You to help me with _____."
4. **Listening** – Sit in silence. Breathe. "Lord, I'm listening."
5. Intercession – "Lord, I lift up _____ today."
6. **Scripture** – Read a Psalm and respond. "Lord, this verse reminds me that _____."
7. **Celebration** – "Lord, You are good because _____."

You don't have to be eloquent. You just have to show up.
  Practice won't make you perfect.
  But it will make you **consistent**.
  And consistency will make you **strong**.

4

Chapter 4 – Learning the Playbook: Praying with Purpose and Variety

In football, a great quarterback doesn't just know how to throw a spiral—he knows **when** to call the right play. First and goal? One play. Third and long? Another. And sometimes? The defense throws something unexpected, and the QB has to call an audible. That's why every great team has a **playbook**—a set of designed responses for different situations.

Prayer works the same way.

You don't pray the same when you're worshiping as you do when you're grieving. You don't pray the same when you're celebrating as you do when someone you love is hurting. In this chapter, we're going to learn to call the right play for the right moment—by expanding our understanding of **different types of prayer**.

Welcome to the Broadcast Booth

Before we dive into the playbook, I thought it might help to call in a little backup from the booth. That's right—we've got our own **spiritual broadcast team** here to help us break down each of the prayer plays like it's Sunday afternoon.

Joining us today:

Hal Michaels –

A legendary play-by-play guy who's called everything from Red Sea partings to goal-line stands in Galatians. Known for his steady narration and uncanny ability to spot a missed prayer opportunity from 50 yards out. If it happens in prayer, Hal will see it, name it, and narrate it like it's on national TV.

Troy Roman –

A former spiritual MVP turned color commentator. Troy knows what it's like to fumble a quiet time, call an audible mid-prayer, and still get the win. Equal parts insightful and unpredictable, Troy brings the real-world experience of a seasoned prayer warrior with a little bit of flair.

Throughout this chapter, we'll be **"throwing it to the booth"** to help you not just understand what kind of prayer you're praying—but why it matters, when to use it, and how to run it with confidence.

So buckle up. The headset's on, the plays are drawn, and the Holy Spirit's got the clipboard.

Let's head down to the field and start calling some prayers.

The Praise Play – Prayer of Adoration

Play Call: Think touchdown celebrations—Billy "White Shoes" Johnson high-stepping, or Deion Sanders dancing into the end zone with that million-dollar smile. That's the energy of adoration prayer.

This isn't about asking God for anything. It's just standing in awe, recognizing who He is, and celebrating His greatness.

Scripture – Psalm 150:6 (NLT):
"Let everything that breathes sing praises to the Lord!"

Booth Commentary

Hal: "We're opening the game with a Praise Play. You can feel the momentum already."

Troy: "This is pure celebration, Hal. Psalm 150 is the spiritual end zone dance—it's telling every living thing to get up and glorify. No requests, no complaints—just admiration. When your prayers start with praise, it puts God in His rightful place and your problems in their proper perspective."

Drawing Up the Play:

- **Purpose:** To reorient your heart around who God is, not what you need.
- **When to Run It:** In moments of joy, peace, or when you feel stuck and need a perspective shift.
- **How to Start It:** "God, You are..." then list His attributes: holy, faithful, powerful, good.
- **Pro Tip:** Make it loud. Sing if you can. Dance if you want.

This is your spiritual end zone moment and when you score a touchdown the refs raise the hands, so don't be afraid to join them.

The Turnover Play – Prayer of Confession

Play Call: Let's talk redemption. Remember that game when **Tony Romo** threw **five interceptions** against the Bills? Total disaster. But somehow—somehow—he led the Cowboys to a last-minute comeback win. That's grace.

Confession is your turnover play. You fumbled. You threw it to the wrong team. But you get another drive.

Scripture – 1 John 1:9 (NLT):

"But if we confess our sins to him, he is faithful and just to forgive us our sins and to cleanse us from all wickedness."

Booth Commentary

Hal: "Oof. We've got a big turnover here—looks like a costly one."

Troy: "That's the thing about confession, Hal. It's not the end—it's the reset. That verse isn't about staying guilty. It's about being cleansed. The Greek word for 'confess' here is *homologeo*—to agree with God about our sin. When we come clean, we don't just get a slap on the wrist—we get restoration. That's how you recover from a spiritual pick-six."

Drawing Up the Play:

- **Purpose:** To be honest with God, realign with grace, and experience spiritual reset.
- **When to Run It:** Anytime you're convicted, weighed down, or after a spiritual "fumble."
- **How to Start It:** "Lord, I confess…" and be specific. Don't sugarcoat. He knows the details.
- **Pro Tip:** Confession isn't about staying ashamed—it's about walking free. Grace is the next play.

The Sideline Check-In – Prayer of Listening

Play Call: Roger Staubach once told a story about calling timeout in a tight game. He went to Coach **Tom Landry** for the next play and found him staring through the hole in the roof of Texas Stadium. Roger said, "So *that's* where you get the plays."

Sometimes you don't need to move—you need to listen.

Scripture – Psalm 46:10 (NLT):
"Be still, and know that I am God."

Booth Commentary

Hal: "Timeout on the field—he's heading to the sideline."

Troy: "This one's about stillness, Hal. Not panic. That verse is an invitation to stop striving and remember who's in control. The Hebrew root of 'be still' actually means to let go, to loosen your grip. Listening prayer is spiritual surrender in action. It's where the best plays get drawn because we finally shut up long enough to hear the Coach."

Drawing Up the Play:

- **Purpose:** To give God space to speak and lead, not just respond.
- **When to Run It:** When you feel lost, pressured, or unsure.
- **How to Start It:** Sit silently for 2–3 minutes. Ask: "Lord, what do You want me to hear today?"
- **Pro Tip:** Journal what comes to mind—even if it's one sentence. Learn to recognize the Shepherd's voice.

The Screen Pass – Prayer of Thanksgiving

Play Call: In football, the screen pass is designed to catch an overly aggressive defense off guard. You let them rush in, thinking they're about to get the sack, then flip the ball over their heads to a running back with blockers in front.

Thanksgiving prayer does the same thing. Life rushes at you—and gratitude flips the script.

Scripture – 1 Thessalonians 5:18 (NLT):
"Be thankful in all circumstances, for this is God's will for you who belong to Christ Jesus."

Booth Commentary

Hal: "Pressure coming up the middle, but wait—he's dumping it off short!"

Troy: "That's textbook, Hal. That verse isn't about pretending

20

everything's fine. It's about perspective. 'Be thankful in all circumstances'—not for all circumstances. Thanksgiving in prayer is the screen pass that softens the blow and keeps you moving forward when life blitzes. Gratitude reroutes your focus from chaos to Christ."

Drawing Up the Play:

- **Purpose:** To ground yourself in what God has already done.
- **When to Run It:** When you're anxious, frustrated, or feeling lack.
- **How to Start It:** "Lord, thank You for..." and name 3 things—even small ones.
- **Pro Tip:** Gratitude isn't about ignoring problems—it's about remembering who solves them.

The Blitz Prayer – Intercession

Play Call: When someone else is under spiritual attack, we run the Blitz Prayer. Think **Lawrence Taylor**—a linebacker who hit so hard quarterbacks needed therapy. You didn't just game-plan around him; you prayed around him.

When life hits someone you love, it's time to step in and pray hard on their behalf.

Scripture – James 5:16 (NLT):

"Pray for each other so that you may be healed. The earnest prayer of a righteous person has great power and produces wonderful results."

Booth Commentary

Hal: "We've got a teammate under pressure—looks like he's dialing up the blitz protection."

Troy: "James 5:16 is big-league, Hal. The word 'earnest' here in Greek—*energeō*—means active, energized prayer. This isn't whisper-in-the-corner prayer. This is step-in-front-of-the-hit, shout-to-heaven prayer. When someone can't stand, we kneel for them. That's what makes the Church the ultimate offensive line."

Drawing Up the Play:

- **Purpose:** To bring someone else before God with boldness and love.
- **When to Run It:** When others are hurting, afraid, or under attack.
- **How to Start It:** "Lord, I lift up [Name] to You. Please..."
- **Pro Tip:** Let them know you're praying. A text or call can make someone feel less alone in the storm.

The Hail Mary – Supplication (Desperate Prayer)

Play Call: In 1975, the Cowboys were trailing the Vikings in a playoff game. With seconds left, Roger Staubach launched a deep ball to Drew Pearson. Pearson made the catch, scored the touchdown, and the Cowboys won.

After the game, Staubach, a Catholic, said, "I closed my eyes and said a **Hail Mary**." That's how the term entered football history—and Christian vocabulary in one pass.

Scripture – Psalm 18:6 (NLT):

"But in my distress I cried out to the Lord; yes, I prayed to my God for help. He heard me from his sanctuary; my cry to him reached his ears."

Booth Commentary

Hal: "We've got a last-second heave going up—he let it fly."

Troy: "And that, Hal, is a textbook Hail Mary prayer. Psalm 18 is David crying from the bottom. The word for 'distress' means being hemmed in—surrounded. But David didn't whisper from the shadows. He cried out. And God didn't ignore him. His cry *reached the sanctuary*. These prayers are born in desperation—but they land in glory."

Drawing Up the Play:

- **Purpose:** To cry out with desperation and surrender.
- **When to Run It:** When the situation is urgent and human solutions are gone.
- **How to Start It:** "God, I need You to..." or simply, "Help."
- **Pro Tip:** Don't wait for a crisis to practice surrender. Use these moments to draw near, not retreat.

The Audible – Spirit-Led Prayer

Play Call: Quarterbacks call an audible when they approach the line, read the defense, and realize the original play won't work. **Peyton Manning** was a master at this. You'd hear him yelling "Omaha! Omaha!"—and next thing you know, the defense is guessing and the offense is rolling.

Spirit-led prayer is your spiritual audible. You had a plan—but God had something better.

Scripture – Romans 8:14 (NLT):

"For all who are led by the Spirit of God are children of God."

Booth Commentary

Hal: "He's changing the call at the line, folks—he's seen something the defense didn't show before."

Troy: "That's the Spirit at work, Hal. Romans 8:14 reminds us—sons and daughters of God aren't just rule followers. They're led. That means mid-prayer, mid-day, mid-life, we stay flexible. The Holy Spirit isn't calling us to repetition; He's calling us to relationship. Some of the best moments in prayer come when we ditch the script."

Drawing Up the Play:

- **Purpose:** To respond to the Spirit's prompting and join God's work in real-time.
- **When to Run It:** When you feel an unexpected prompting or encounter a surprise need.
- **How to Start It:** "Lord, what are You doing right now—and

how can I be part of it?"

- **Pro Tip:** Keep a flexible heart. Some of your most powerful prayers will come when the play changes.

Prayer Drill #3: Build Your Weekly Playbook

Pick a different play to run each day this week:

- **Monday** – Praise Day – Adoration and Focus
- **Tuesday** – Turnover Play - Confession
- **Wednesday** – Sideline Check-In – Listening
- **Thursday** – Screen Pass – Thanksgiving
- **Friday** – Blitz Play – Intercession
- **Saturday** – Hail Mary – Supplication
- **Sunday** – Audible – Spirit-led Prayer

Your challenge this week is not to pray perfectly.

It's to pray **intentionally**.

Learn the playbook. Run the right plays.

And trust the Coach who sees the whole field.

5

Chapter 5 – Getting in Game Shape: Strengthening Your Prayer Muscles

In sports, no one shows up to the championship out of shape and expects to win. They train. They condition. They build strength, focus, and endurance long before they ever hit the big stage. The same is true in prayer.

But if we're being honest, most of us try to "win" in prayer without ever preparing for it. We go in cold. We fumble through five distracted minutes. We lose track of what we were praying about. And we wonder why it doesn't feel powerful.

Prayer isn't performance—but it does require **preparation**.

That's what this chapter is all about: **getting in game shape.** Developing prayer stamina, strategy, and strength so that when life throws you into a spiritual battle, you don't just survive— you're ready.

The Booth Is Back

Hal Michaels: "We're back in the booth training camp, and let me tell you, these guys are working hard,"

Troy Roman: "That's right, Hal. This chapter is all about training camp. We're moving past the playbook and into the grind. This is where good intentions meet discipline. And discipline? That's where greatness is born.

And speaking of greatness, let me tell you—we've brought in a legend to walk us through this season. You want training? You want results? Then you need **Coach Blaze**. This guy has trained spiritual warriors across generations. He doesn't pull punches, and he doesn't waste time. Get ready, because Blaze is stepping onto the field, and he's about to show us how to get in game shape."

Author's Note: I hated workouts. I liked being strong. I liked making the team. But dragging myself back into the weight room after being sore from the last session? Miserable. Still, I did it. Because I wanted to be great.

That's how I feel about prayer. I want to be a Hall of Fame Prayer Warrior. But that kind of spiritual fitness doesn't happen by accident. I've got to get in prayer shape.

NFL legend Jerry Rice once said, "Today I will do what others won't, so tomorrow I can do what others can't." That's prayer training. It's the stuff behind the scenes—early, quiet, even painful—that turns a casual Christian into a spiritual champion.

SECTION 1 – TRAINING FOR PRAYER: BUILDING THE FOUNDATION

Prayer is not just knowing *what* to say—it's building the internal strength and discipline to *keep showing up*. Just like an athlete doesn't improve with one great play, your prayer life won't grow from one great prayer. It grows from training—intentional, daily, often unseen, always valuable.

Here are the foundational components of getting in game shape:

1. Prayer Endurance – Stretching Your Capacity to Stay in the Game

Scripture: Luke 18:1 – "One day Jesus told his disciples a story to show that they should always pray and never give up."

Building endurance in prayer is like training for a marathon—you start with small, consistent stretches and build over time. Many people give up too early because they're not conditioned to press on. Jesus taught us not to quit, even when we feel dry. Endurance is a muscle we train through repetition.

Why We Struggle: We get discouraged when we feel like our prayers aren't effective or emotional. But Jesus Himself taught us to keep going—to *not give up*. It's not about eloquence or how much you feel—it's about persistence.

Drill – Interval Expansion:

1. Start with 5 minutes of focused prayer time daily.
2. Break it into simple intervals:

• 1 minute adoration (praising God)

- 1 minute confession (clearing your heart)
- 1 minute thanksgiving (gratitude)
- 2 minutes supplication (praying for needs)

1. Add one minute every three days.
2. Track your time in a notebook or journal.

💡 **Note:** If you're not sure what to say or how to structure this, the **ACTS Prayer Method** is your best friend. If you check out the Appendix, we have additional information about this Method. You can download the free ACTS guide at https://disciplebluepr int.com/wp-content/uploads/2024/10/ACTS-Prayer-Method-Worksheet-1.pdf and keep it beside your Bible.

This is about developing spiritual endurance. Just like running gets easier the more you do it, so does prayer.

2. Mental Toughness – Focusing When the Fog Sets In

Scripture: Colossians 4:2 – "Devote yourselves to prayer with an alert mind and a thankful heart."

Prayer takes focus, and focus takes training. Our minds are flooded daily with distractions that challenge our ability to stay spiritually sharp. Mental toughness in prayer means carving out clarity, pushing past mental clutter, and choosing presence over passivity. Like a muscle, your focus gets stronger every time you practice it.

Why We Struggle: The world is noisy—so are our thoughts. Notifications, to-do lists, and wandering minds can derail even the most earnest prayer time.

Drill – The Prayer Zone Routine:

1. **Designate a place.** Make it your prayer spot—your porch, a chair, a closet.
2. **Silence distractions.** Phone off or in another room. No screens.
3. **Set a short focus timer.** Start with 5–7 minutes to build discipline. (Okay, maybe your phone needs to stay on for this—but make sure it's on silent mode. No buzzing distractions.)
4. **Use physical anchors.** A candle, a prayer journal, or a favorite devotional book that signals "this is prayer time."
5. **Brain Dump First.** Write down everything on your mind so you can release it.

Coach Blaze Insight: "You can't run plays if your mind's still in the locker room. Focus isn't natural—it's trained. Don't expect clarity if you haven't cleared space."

3. Spiritual Strength – Showing Up When You Don't Feel Like It

Scripture: 1 Timothy 4:7-8 – "Train yourself to be godly. Physical training is good, but training for godliness is much better..."

We often equate spiritual strength with deep emotion or powerful moments, but true strength is showing up when we don't feel anything at all. This is where discipline trumps desire. When you keep showing up in the dry seasons, you're building strength that doesn't depend on feeling—it depends on faith.

Prayer isn't just for when you feel inspired. It's a discipline, not just a desire. The strongest spiritual lives are built by people who choose to show up on days they don't feel like it.

Why We Struggle: We associate spiritual strength with emotional highs. But real strength is forged when we persist through spiritual lows.

Drill – The 21-Day Repetition Challenge:

1. Commit to a set time to pray for the next 21 days (morning, lunch, bedtime—pick what works).
2. Keep it manageable—5 to 10 minutes is fine.
3. Use a tracker. Every day you show up, mark it down.
4. Reflect briefly: What was hard? What helped? What felt different?

💡 **Coach Blaze Insight:** "You build strength when no one's watching. When your knees hit the floor even when your heart's not in it—*that's training.*"

4. Recovery and Rhythm – Rest Is Part of the Training Plan

Scripture: Isaiah 40:31 – "But those who trust in the Lord will find new strength..."

Great athletes know rest isn't weakness—it's how you build back stronger. The same goes for your prayer life. God created rest as part of the rhythm of life. When we trust Him enough to pause, He renews our strength. It's not just about praying hard—it's also about learning to pause well.

Even the best athletes rest. Without recovery, they crash. Spiritually, we often forget that *rhythm* matters. God built cycles of work and rest into creation—and into us.

Why We Struggle: We equate spirituality with constant activity. But Sabbath, silence, and solitude are all spiritual disciplines, too.

Drill – Sabbath Signal:

1. Choose one day per week to change the pace. No tasks. No checklists. Just connection.
2. Spend time with God in unhurried ways: walk in nature, listen to worship, journal your thoughts.
3. Take a nap—yes, really. Rest reminds us we're not God.

Bonus Micro Drill – Prayer Breathers:
Add short pauses in your day to breathe and re-center.

- Before a meeting: "God, give me wisdom."
- While waiting: "Lord, I'm listening."
- After an argument: "Father, help me respond, not react."

Coach Blaze Insight: "Sabbath isn't weakness—it's wisdom. You don't just need fuel to run—you need brakes to finish the race."

Bonus Drill - Always in the Game (1 Thessalonians 5:17)

Scripture: "Never stop praying." (1 Thessalonians 5:17)

This verse isn't about nonstop talking—it's about staying spiritually alert and available. It's like keeping your headset on during the whole game. Prayer can become a reflex, a quiet habit throughout your day. The more you stay tuned in, the easier it becomes to pray instantly, naturally, and effectively in any moment.

Drill – Whispered Prayer Breaks:

1. Set 3–5 reminders during your day (use your phone or sticky notes).
2. When the reminder pops, whisper a quick prayer:

- "Lord, guide me."
- "Thank You for this moment."
- "Help me be aware of You."

1. Over time, this develops a prayerful mindset that becomes second nature.

Coach Blaze Insight: "Real champions don't wait for game time to listen—they're on headset all day."

SECTION 2 - POSITION DRILLS: TRAINING FOR EACH PRAYER TYPE

Now that you've trained your heart and mind, let's work on the drills that develop your **spiritual agility** in each type of prayer.

Each prayer type is a vital part of your game. Neglect one, and your prayer life can feel unbalanced, unpracticed, and ultimately unfruitful. These aren't just concepts—they're tools you'll need when the game gets intense. These drills help you stay sharp, grounded, and equipped in every situation.

Kobe Bryant once shocked his Olympic teammates by getting up at 4 a.m. to train—*before* their team workout. One teammate said, "While we were sleeping, he was working." That's the kind of commitment we're after—not legalism, but passion.

And as Paul said in 1 Corinthians 9:27 (NLT), *"I discipline my body like an athlete, training it to do what it should."* Prayer is part of that discipline—it's our spiritual gym.

33

Each prayer type includes:

- Coach Blaze Motivation – why this play matters and what happens if we neglect it
- Scripture – included directly in the text
- Breakdown – deeper explanation of the prayer type's purpose
- Drill – actionable training
- Next-Level Growth – guidance to move from beginner to all-pro

Adoration (Praise Play)

Coach Blaze: "Praise isn't optional—it's your anthem, your kickoff, your alignment. If you skip it, you risk starting the game distracted and self-focused. Praise resets the field. It magnifies God and minimizes everything else."

Scripture: *"I will exalt you, my God and King, and praise your name forever and ever. I will praise you every day; yes, I will praise you forever. Great is the Lord! He is most worthy of praise!"* – Psalm 145:1–3 (NLT)

Breakdown: Praise is a declaration of who God is, not a reflection of how we feel. It places God on the throne of our hearts and repositions our circumstances in light of His greatness. When we begin with praise, we move from anxiety to awe, from worry to worship, and from self-focus to Christ-focus.

Drill:

- Start every prayer this week with 60 seconds of praise.
- Use a list of God's attributes: "God, You are holy... just... faithful..."
- Speak it aloud—even if alone. Praise shifts your posture.

Next-Level Growth:

- **Benchwarmer** – Begin each prayer with a single statement of praise like "God, You are good."
- **Starter** – Create a short daily praise list using the ACTS method.
- **All-Pro** – Memorize and recite full psalms of praise. Lead others in adoration prayers.

Confession (Turnover Play)

Coach Blaze: "You want to know what stalls a prayer life faster than anything else? Unconfessed sin. When you carry guilt onto the field, it weighs you down, clouds your confidence, and dulls your focus. Confession is your turnover recovery. Don't carry it—clear it."

Scripture: *"But if we confess our sins to him, he is faithful and just to forgive us our sins and to cleanse us from all wickedness."* – 1 John 1:9 (NLT)

Breakdown: Confession restores what sin disrupts—our intimacy with God. Sin doesn't cancel our salvation, but it does damage our closeness with the Father. When we confess, we invite His grace into our failure, and we rebuild the relational bridge that sin has weakened. Forgiveness is certain, but repentance is what restores connection.

Drill:

- Keep a journal called "Turnover Tracker."
- Write one area of failure.
- Then write a promise (from Psalms, Romans 8, etc.) next to it.

Next-Level Growth:

- **Benchwarmer** – Write one confession a week and ask God for forgiveness.
- **Starter** – Confess daily and pair it with a scripture of grace.
- **All-Pro** – Develop a rhythm of immediate confession. Help others walk in restoration.

Listening (Sideline Check-In)

Coach Blaze: "Some of you keep asking God for answers, but you're not stopping long enough to hear the reply. Listening isn't passive—it's powerful. If you skip this, you'll end up running the wrong plays. This is where direction is received and relationships are deepened."

Scripture: *"My sheep listen to my voice; I know them, and they follow me."* – John 10:27 (NLT)

Breakdown: God speaks, but often we miss His voice because our lives are too noisy. Listening prayer cultivates awareness of God's presence and trains our spiritual ears to recognize His guidance. It's how we move from self-driven prayers to Spirit-led alignment, receiving wisdom that we didn't even know we needed.

Coach Blaze Insight: "If you're always talking, you can't hear the coach call the next play. Silence isn't awkward—it's strategic. Learn to love it."

God speaks, but often we miss His voice because our lives are too noisy and we aren't paying attention or looking for the answer. Listening prayer cultivates awareness of God's presence and trains our spiritual ears to recognize His guidance. It's how we move from self-driven prayers to Spirit-led alignment, receiving wisdom that we didn't even know we needed.

Drill:

- Set a 5-minute timer.
- Ask one question: "Lord, what do You want me to know today?"
- Sit in silence. Jot down any scripture, word, or nudge you sense.

Next-Level Growth:

- **Benchwarmer** – Pause at the end of your prayer and listen for 30 seconds.
- **Starter** – Add 5 minutes of listening to each prayer session.
- **All-Pro** – Journal daily insights and test them against scripture. Teach others to hear God's voice.

Thanksgiving (Screen Pass)

Coach Blaze: "When life sends a full-on blitz, thanksgiving is how you survive the hit. If you neglect gratitude, frustration will take over. This is your screen pass—your spiritual safety valve that changes everything."

Scripture: *"Be thankful in all circumstances, for this is God's will for you who belong to Christ Jesus."* – 1 Thessalonians 5:18 (NLT)

Breakdown: Thanksgiving refocuses our hearts and trains us to see God's goodness even when life is hard. It breaks the power of negativity and renews our hope. The discipline of gratitude changes the atmosphere of our hearts, reminding us that God is still at work—especially when it's not obvious.

Drill:

- Start or end every prayer with 3 new things you're thankful for.
- Keep a running list. Review it when you feel overwhelmed.

Next-Level Growth:

- **Benchwarmer** – Say "Thank You" for one thing during prayer.
- **Starter** – Keep a gratitude list in your journal.
- **All-Pro** – Express thanksgiving in difficult moments. Lead a group in shared praise.

Intercession (Blitz Prayer)

Coach Blaze: "When your teammate's getting hit, you step in front of the attack. That's intercession. Don't underestimate this play—it's powerful. Neglect it, and someone else carries weight you were meant to lift."

Scripture: *"The earnest prayer of a righteous person has great power and produces wonderful results."* – James 5:16 (NLT)

Breakdown: Intercession is spiritual advocacy. It's standing in the gap for others with intentional, faith-filled prayer. This type of prayer calls down heaven's resources into someone else's situation. It's the heartbeat of selfless love—moving beyond "what do I need?" to "what do they need?" and trusting God to move mightily.

Drill:

- Create a Prayer Roster: name, need, and date.
- Assign one person per day.
- After praying, shoot them a quick message: "I prayed for you today."

Next-Level Growth:

- **Benchwarmer** – Pray for one person per week.
- **Starter** – Keep a rotating list of family, friends, and church needs.
- **All-Pro** – Intercede daily, follow up with others, and lead group intercession.

Supplication (Hail Mary)

Coach Blaze: "You're out of time. No timeouts left. You launch one last shot toward heaven. That's supplication. When life collapses, this is the play you need ready. If you never practice crying out, don't expect composure when crisis comes."

Scripture: *"But in my distress I cried out to the Lord; yes, I prayed to my God for help. He heard me from his sanctuary; my cry to him reached his ears."* – Psalm 18:6 (NLT)

Breakdown: Supplication is the prayer of the desperate—raw, unfiltered, and faith-driven. These aren't rehearsed words; they're cries from the soul. In these moments, we discover the nearness and responsiveness of God, who hears and moves not because our words are fancy, but because our hearts are surrendered.

Drill:

- Write 3 one-line "crisis prayers" and memorize them.
- In your hardest moments, fire them off.
- Trust that your Hail Mary didn't hit the ground.

Next-Level Growth:

- **Benchwarmer** – Memorize one simple prayer for when you feel overwhelmed.
- **Starter** – Use short prayers in moments of fear or anxiety.
- **All-Pro** – Combine scripture with crisis prayers and teach others how to cry out in faith.

Spirit-Led Prayer (The Audible)

Coach Blaze: "Sometimes the Spirit calls a last-second audible. You had a plan—God had a better one. If you don't stay open to this, you'll miss divine appointments. Flexibility in prayer is how we follow a living, leading God."

Scripture: *"For all who are led by the Spirit of God are children of God."* – Romans 8:14 (NLT)

Breakdown: Spirit-led prayer is about surrendering our agenda in favor of God's. It means adjusting your prayer in real-time as the Holy Spirit nudges your heart. This level of prayer is deeply relational, rooted in attentiveness and trust that God sees more than we do—and knows just what needs to be prayed.

Drill:

- Begin each prayer time with: "Holy Spirit, what do You want me to pray today?"
- Don't resist the nudge—follow it.
- Keep a log of answered Spirit-led prayers.

Next-Level Growth:

- **Benchwarmer** – Ask the Holy Spirit one question in prayer this week.
- **Starter** – Practice listening daily and praying spontaneously.
- **All-Pro** – Submit your whole prayer list to the Spirit. Model flexibility in group prayer settings.

41

CLOSING CHALLENGE – YOUR 7-DAY PRAYER TRAINING PLAN

Here's your first spiritual workout plan. Fill it out and commit to it this week:

Example:

- Day: Monday
- Time: 7:00 a.m. before leaving for work
- Focus: Family (Spouse, children, parents)
- Method Notes: Pray individually for each family member by name, Thank God for them. Ask for their protection spiritual growth, and encouragement today.

Monday:

- Time I will pray: _____
- Focus of prayer: _____
- Method notes/reminder: _____

Tuesday:

- Time I will pray: _____
- Focus of prayer: _____
- Method notes/reminder: _____

Wednesday:

- Time I will pray: _____
- Focus of prayer: _____
- Method notes/reminder: _____

Thursday:

- Time I will pray: _____
- Focus of prayer: _____
- Method notes/reminder: _____

Friday:

- Time I will pray: _____
- Focus of prayer: _____
- Method notes/reminder: _____

Saturday:

- Time I will pray: _____
- Focus of prayer: _____
- Method notes/reminder: _____

Sunday:

- Time I will pray: _____
- Focus of prayer: _____
- Method notes/reminder: _____

Download a printable version of the ACTS guide at https://discip leblueprint.com/wp-content/uploads/2024/10/ACTS-Prayer-Method-Worksheet-1.pdf.

"Champions don't become champions in the ring—they are merely recognized there." – Joe Frazier

Train like it matters. Because it does. Show up. Get stronger. Trust your Coach.

6

Chapter 6: Drawing Up the Victory Plan

Hal Michaels: "We're back in the booth for pregame coverage of the spiritual season, and let me tell you, this one's not for casual fans."

Author's Note: Abraham Lincoln once said, "Give me six hours to chop down a tree and I will spend the first four sharpening the axe." It's a principle we forget in prayer. We want power without preparation. Breakthrough without a plan. But if you want victory on the field, your strategy has to start before the whistle blows.

Every good coach knows the importance of "The Script." Before kickoff, many teams prepare their first 15–20 offensive plays in advance. They're not guessing—they're executing a plan. Why? Because when the crowd is loud and the pressure's high, emotion can cloud judgment. Prayer works the same way. If you wait until you're overwhelmed to decide how to pray, chances are you won't pray with confidence—you'll pray with confusion.

I've lived that out. There was a season in my life where I

committed to pray more, but I never made a plan. And just like skipping leg day, I ended up skipping prayer day—over and over. I wasn't lazy, I was just aimless. It wasn't until I started treating prayer like a strategy that I started gaining traction.

Troy Roman: "And speaking of preparation, we've got a legend joining us again on the field—Coach Blaze. He's the guy who turns good intentions into real game-time readiness."

Coach Blaze Insight: "You don't show up on game day flipping through random plays. A great team knows what to run—and when to run it. Same with prayer."

1. Why Spontaneous Prayer Isn't Enough

Coach Blaze Insight: "Showing up unprepared might cut it in a backyard scrimmage—but not when you're stepping into the presence of the King. Come with a game plan. Show Him He matters."

Spontaneous prayer is a gift—it's how we stay connected to God in the moment. But without structure, prayer often becomes reactive, shallow, or neglected altogether. No team goes into a big game without a strategy. Why would we walk into a spiritual battle without one?

Imagine telling the Coach you have some ideas to improve the defense. He's intrigued and sets up a meeting with you and the Defensive Coordinator. Would you just go in and wing it? I wouldn't. I'd be prepared. I'd have plays drawn up, statistics to support my recommendations, and I'd treat it like the opportunity of a lifetime.

And yet—how often do we walk into a meeting with God

unprepared? When we go to God in prayer, we are entering the throne room. We are meeting with our Maker, our Savior, and our King. And sometimes, I treat that sacred privilege more casually than I would a meeting with a football coach. It's humbling to admit, but it's true.

Think about this: Jesus, the Son of God, often retreated to pray intentionally. He had rhythms. He prayed early in the morning (Mark 1:35), before making big decisions (Luke 6:12–13), and even while in agony (Luke 22:41–44). His prayer life was planned and powerful.

If we want to grow, we need to stop treating prayer like a backup plan—and start treating it like our primary weapon.

2. Building Your Weekly Prayer Game Plan

Coach Blaze Insight: "Preparation isn't just for game day—it's for every day. If you don't schedule time with God, the enemy will schedule something else for you."

Here's how to build a weekly prayer game plan:

Monday – Family

Pray for your spouse, children, parents, siblings, extended family. Cover their health, relationships, faith, jobs, and struggles. Lift up their marriages, their spiritual growth, and the unity of your household. Ask God to protect, provide, and guide your family with wisdom and grace.

Tuesday – Friends

Lift up your close friends, coworkers, neighbors, and those you've been meaning to reconnect with. Pray for their physical and emotional needs. Ask God to deepen the friendships that bring life, and give you discernment about ones that need boundaries or healing.

Wednesday – Church & Ministry

Pray for your pastor, leadership team, small groups, Sunday school teachers, worship leaders, and volunteers. Intercede for unity, clear vision, and spiritual fruit. Pray for the unsaved who walk through the doors and the faithful who carry the burdens of others.

Thursday – Community & Nation

Pray for local schools, law enforcement, hospitals, city leaders, and businesses. Then widen your circle to national issues: government leaders, national revival, cultural conflicts, and justice. Ask God to intervene in ways only He can.

Friday – Missions & Global Concerns

Intercede for missionaries around the world—those in dangerous places and those in discouraging ones. Pray for unreached people groups, persecuted Christians, and major global events. Ask God to open doors, raise up workers, and use you to support His mission.

Saturday – Spiritual Growth

Ask God to grow you. Bring Him your fears, your flaws, and your desires. Pray about your calling, your temptations, and your daily disciplines. Ask Him to refine your character, strengthen your gifts, and help you grow in wisdom and boldness.

Sunday – Praise & Listening

Don't bring a list—bring your attention. Spend time praising God for who He is. Reflect on the past week. Then sit in silence and ask, "Lord, what do You want to show me?" Let Sunday be your spiritual reset.

Use a journal or whiteboard to track wins, breakthroughs, and lingering burdens. Create a repeatable rhythm—like 10 minutes in the morning and 5 minutes at night.

A game plan helps prayer become a lifestyle, not just a last resort.

3. Scouting the Enemy (Spiritual Warfare)

Coach Blaze Insight: "You wouldn't face a linebacker like Micah Parson's without studying tape. So why do you try to battle the enemy without knowing his schemes?"

Troy Roman: "And let's be clear—this isn't a scrimmage. You're not just out here running routes for fun. This is a full-contact battle for your soul, your mind, and your family. And if you don't prepare, you're going to get blindsided."

Scripture tells us that we're in a battle—not against flesh and blood, but against spiritual forces (Ephesians 6:12). Satan's tactics include distraction, discouragement, delay, and deception. He studies you. He watches your film. He knows your weaknesses—and if you think he's going to take it easy on you because you had a quiet time last week, think again.

That's why the Bible tells us to put on the **armor of God**—not just once, but daily. Think of it like a football uniform:

- **Helmet of Salvation** – Protects your mind. Know who you belong to. The enemy will attack your identity.

49

- **Breastplate of Righteousness** – Guards your heart. Living right doesn't save you, but it keeps your conscience clean.
- **Belt of Truth** – Holds everything together. Without truth, you have nothing firm to stand on.
- **Shoes of Peace** – Give you footing. In chaos, you stay grounded.
- **Shield of Faith** – Blocks fiery darts. Doubts, accusations, temptations—you need faith to deflect them.
- **Sword of the Spirit** – The Word of God. You don't just block the enemy—you strike back.

Coach Blaze Insight: "You don't suit up halfway and expect to win. The enemy doesn't take days off, and neither should your armor."

Include this in your prayer strategy:

- **Ephesians 6 Armor Checks** – Pray through the armor of God daily, piece by piece.
- **Scripture Arsenal** – Memorize verses that confront your battles: fear, anger, lust, anxiety.
- **Emergency Audibles** – Prepare short, direct prayers you can use when temptation hits hard.

Prayer isn't just communion—it's combat. You're not praying to feel better. You're praying to stand firm, push back darkness, and protect the territory God's entrusted to you.

4. Team Strategy (Prayer Partners & Groups)

Coach Blaze Insight: "Even the best players don't win games alone. You need teammates who have your back in prayer—people who cover your blind spots, pick you up, and keep you focused when your faith feels shaky."

Even the greatest quarterbacks need teammates.

Ecclesiastes 4:12 (NLT) says, "A person standing alone can be attacked and defeated, but two can stand back-to-back and conquer. Three are even better, for a triple-braided cord is not easily broken."

That's not just true in battle—it's true in prayer. You weren't meant to pray alone all the time. Jesus had Peter, James, and John in Gethsemane. Paul constantly asked churches to pray for him.

Team Prayer Benefits:

- Accountability
- Strength in agreement (Matthew 18:19–20)
- Discernment through shared wisdom

Build Your Team:

- Choose 1–2 trusted believers for regular check-ins
- Join a group text or prayer chain
- Schedule monthly group prayer nights

Coach Blaze Insight: "A lone player gets picked off. A team watches each other's blind spots."

5. Red Zone Strategy (Crisis & Urgent Prayer)

Coach Blaze Insight: "In the red zone, there's no time for overthinking—you run the play you've trained for. That's why preparation matters. Your crisis prayers shouldn't be your first reps—they should be your most practiced ones."

Troy Roman: "For those less familiar with football lingo, the 'red zone' is that critical area inside the opponent's 20-yard line. It's where scoring gets tougher, the pressure ramps up, and mistakes are magnified. It's crunch time—and you better have the right play ready."

What do you do when the pressure is on? Crisis prayers aren't the time to figure out your theology—they're the time to lean into your trust.

In the Red Zone, you need:

- One-line prayers you've practiced (Psalm 18:6 style)
- Scriptures memorized that anchor your emotions
- A pre-made short list of people you can call/text to pray immediately

Don't wait for panic to prepare. You're in the red zone—call the right play.

6. Timeouts and Halftime (Rest & Realignment)

Coach Blaze Insight: "Every sport has a built-in break—halftime in football and basketball, the seventh-inning stretch in baseball, even 15-minute intermissions in hockey. If athletes need time to reset and refocus, why wouldn't disciples?"

Every team needs rest—so do you. God built Sabbath into the rhythm of creation. Your game plan should include space for:

- Silence
- Worship
- Reflection
- Re-evaluation of your spiritual condition

Psalm 46:10 reminds us, "Be still, and know that I am God!" That's not just a poetic suggestion—it's a command that anchors our soul when the noise of life gets too loud. When we rest in God's presence, we're reminded who's in control.

Romans 8:26 also tells us, "And the Holy Spirit helps us in our weakness... the Holy Spirit prays for us with groanings that cannot be expressed in words." Sometimes in rest, when we have no words left, the Spirit fills in the silence with divine intercession.

Timeouts and halftime aren't signs of weakness—they're part of the winning strategy. Step away. Get quiet. Let God reset your heart for what's next.

Every team needs rest—so do you. God built Sabbath into the rhythm of creation. Your game plan should include space for:

- Silence
- Worship
- Reflection
- Re-evaluation of your spiritual condition

Coach Blaze Insight: "Even champions need the bench. Not because they're weak—but because smart players rest when it's time. You're not God. Stop pretending to be."

7. Drawing Up the Prayer Playbook

This section gives you a go-to strategy for each prayer type. These aren't drills (you already worked those in Chapter 5)—these are tactical plays to use in real-life spiritual moments.

Adoration (Praise Play)

When to Use: Start of prayer, spiritual dryness, or moments of awe

Game Plan: Open with who God is—not what you need. Recite scripture-based praise (e.g., Psalm 145). Use a praise playlist, speak attributes aloud, or write a praise letter to God.

Strategy:
Adoration helps you start your prayer from a place of reverence rather than need. It's not about informing God of who He is—it's about reminding *your own heart* who you're speaking to. This realigns your spiritual posture, shifts your focus upward,

and prepares your soul to pray with the right attitude.

Success Indicator:

You'll know it's working when the anxiety that felt so big starts to shrink. When praise softens your pride, sharpens your joy, and gives you perspective. You may not get all the answers, but you'll feel anchored in awe—and that's where all effective prayer begins.

Sample Play:

"God, You are my refuge and strength. You are unchanging when everything else shifts. You are holy, righteous, and full of compassion. I praise You not because my life is easy—but because You are always worthy."

Confession (Turnover Play)

When to Use: After sin, in conviction, or during repentance

Game Plan: Be honest. Name the sin. Pair your confession with a promise of grace (1 John 1:9). Ask God to reveal blind spots. Journaling helps with honesty.

Strategy:

Confession isn't just about acknowledging failure—it's about **reestablishing connection** with God. Sin doesn't remove your salvation, but it does interrupt your intimacy. Confession tears down the wall. And it's not only about the sins we know we've committed (sins of commission), but also the ones we didn't even realize (sins of omission). This kind of prayer allows God to search your heart and bring hidden issues into the light.

Success Indicator:

If you leave your confession still feeling like you're hiding, you may have more to say. But when that weight lifts, peace returns, and you feel clean—like you want to walk back into God's arms instead of hide from Him—that's the fruit of true confession. It frees your spirit to breathe again.

Sample Play:

"Father, I confess that I've been impatient, short-tempered, and selfish this week. I've ignored your prompting and put my comfort above obedience. Forgive me for what I've done—and what I've failed to do. Thank You for your mercy. Cleanse my heart and draw me close again."

Listening (Sideline Check-In)

When to Use: After a decision, during tension, or in quiet time

Game Plan: Ask: "Lord, what do You want me to hear today?" Then wait. Use a timer (yes, even if your phone's on silent mode). Record any impressions, verses, or nudges.

Strategy:

Listening prayer invites God to speak first. It shifts the power dynamic—we stop trying to steer and start receiving. This is where prayer becomes conversation. It's also where we train our ears to recognize God's voice in a world full of noise.

Success Indicator:

When you begin to sense consistent themes in your quiet moments—scripture that sticks, names that surface, nudges you can't shake—that's a sign you're tuning in. It may feel subtle at first, but peace, clarity, and obedience will grow.

Sample Play:

"Lord, I'm quieting my heart now. If there's something You want to say, I'm listening. Help me to hear You—not just with my ears, but with my spirit. Lead me where You want me to go."

Thanksgiving (Screen Pass)

When to Use: In stress, joy, daily review, or answered prayer

Game Plan: List 3 new things every day. Be specific: "Thank You for that conversation," "for a working car," "for the warm sun." Gratitude reroutes frustration and fuels joy.

Strategy:

Thanksgiving trains your heart to see blessings instead of burdens. It reframes your reality and anchors your spirit in God's goodness. In moments of anxiety or loss, it's your spiritual screen pass—a way to slip past heaviness and run forward with trust.

Success Indicator:

If your first instinct becomes thankfulness rather than complaint, you're making progress. Gratitude will lift your focus, soften your heart, and turn ordinary moments into spiritual milestones.

Sample Play:

"Thank You, Lord, for waking me up today. For the cup of coffee. For the encouraging word from a friend. Even in the small things, You are present—and I'm grateful."

Intercession (Blitz Prayer)

When to Use: For others in crisis, healing, salvation, or spiritual breakthrough

Game Plan: Keep a prayer roster. Pray by name and need. Don't be vague—pray boldly. Let them know: "I prayed for you today."

Strategy:

Intercession moves you beyond self. It's spiritual defense and offense for someone else. This is where love takes action— where your burden for others becomes a battlefield of faith. You're not just talking to God about people—you're doing spiritual warfare on their behalf.

Success Indicator:

You'll start to notice your compassion deepening. You'll feel more connected to the people you're praying for. And when they experience peace or breakthrough, you'll know your prayer was part of something powerful.

Sample Play:

"God, I lift up James to You right now. You know his situation—his pain, his doubts, his need for healing. Surround him with peace. Show him that You're near. Work in ways that only You can."

Supplication (Hail Mary)

When to Use: In desperation, loss, fear, or big life moments

Game Plan: Cry out. Use short, Scripture-rooted requests: "God, rescue me." "Lord, be my strength." Keep them written where you can access them fast.

Strategy:

Supplication is your lifeline in crisis. It's raw, unfiltered, and born of need. These prayers strip away pretense and move the heart of God. They are less about eloquence and more about surrender. This is how we cry for help and hold on when nothing makes sense.

Success Indicator:

When your fear is replaced by trust—even if the situation hasn't changed—you'll know your supplication has reached heaven. Sometimes the miracle is external. Other times, it's internal. Either way, you've touched the heart of God.

Sample Play:

"Jesus, I don't know what to do right now. I feel overwhelmed, anxious, and scared. I need You. Be my peace. Carry me through this moment—I trust You, even though I don't understand."

Spirit-Led Prayer (The Audible)

When to Use: When your planned prayer feels redirected

Game Plan: Ask the Spirit to guide. If He brings someone to mind—pray. If a topic keeps resurfacing—press into it. Let the Spirit change the play at the line of scrimmage.

Strategy:
This kind of prayer requires flexibility. You're no longer quarterback—you're receiver. It's about trusting the Spirit to call the play and having the courage to follow where He leads. These moments grow your faith and open doors you never saw coming.

Success Indicator:
When the prayer you didn't plan becomes the one you needed most, or when God uses your words to bless someone in ways you never intended—you're hearing the Spirit and letting Him lead.

Sample Play:
"Holy Spirit, guide me. If I'm missing something—show me. If there's someone I need to pray for—bring them to mind. I'm here, and I'm open. Lead the way."

Final Thoughts

Every strong team wants to move from good to great—and in prayer, the same holds true. Below is a way to visualize your growth and help you measure how you're progressing in your prayer life. Whether you're just getting off the bench or pushing toward spiritual greatness, this table helps you see what next-level effort looks like:

Adoration

- **Off the Bench** - Occasionally says "thank you" to God
- **Starting Player** - Begins prayer with praise regularly
- **Hall of Fame Level** - Has a heart posture rooted in daily worship

Confession

- **Off the Bench** - Only confesses when convicted
- **Starting Player** - Confesses known sin with honesty
- **Hall of Fame Level** - Invites God to reveal hidden sin routinely

Listening

- **Off the Bench** - Rarely sits in silence
- **Starting Player** - Practices silence weekly
- **Hall of Fame Level** - Lives in tune with God's voice daily

Thanksgiving

- **Off the Bench** - Says grace at meals
- **Starting Player** – Thanks God for specifics
- **Hall of Fame Level** - Sees all of life through a gratitude filter

Intercession

- **Off the Bench** - Prays for others occasionally
- **Starting Player** - Maintains a prayer list
- **Hall of Fame Level** - Feels burdened and prays with passion

Supplication

- **Off the Bench** - Prays in emergencies
- **Starting Player** - Prays consistently for personal needs
- **Hall of Fame Level** - Surrenders desires and prays God's will

Spirit-led

- **Off the Bench** - Follows a fixed routine
- **Starting Player** - Open to change when prompted
- **Hall of Fame Level** - Expects and welcomes the Spirit's redirection

And remember:

"Everyone wants the results, but not everyone wants the reps. Prayer warriors are made in the quiet reps no one else sees."
— *Coach Blaze*

Chapter 7: The Comeback

Coach Blaze Insight: "Comebacks don't happen in the highlights—they're born in the locker room, when no one's watching. But they also rise up in hospital rooms when the diagnosis changes everything, and in back alleys where addiction whispers you'll never make it out. If you've been knocked down, now's your moment. Get up. The play clock's still ticking."

Greatest Comebacks in Sports

In 2011, the Dallas Mavericks pulled off one of the greatest NBA Finals comebacks ever. In Game 2, they were down by 15 points with just over 7 minutes left. Against LeBron James, Dwyane Wade, and the star-studded Miami Heat, it looked like the game—and the series—was lost. But Dirk Nowitzki and the Mavs went on a 22–5 run and stole the game in the final seconds. That win shifted momentum and helped Dallas win the championship.

Or take December 17, 2022: the Minnesota Vikings trailed

the Indianapolis Colts 33–0 at halftime. That's not a typo—33 points. The fans were leaving. Social media was roasting them. But they didn't give up. Led by Kirk Cousins, they mounted the greatest comeback in NFL history, winning 39–36 in overtime. No one thought it was possible... until it was.

Comebacks don't start with victory—they start with belief. A flicker of hope. A voice that says, "Get back in the game."

The Anatomy of a Comeback

Comebacks are never easy. In sports, they require belief—faith that even when you're down big, the game isn't over. You don't launch a comeback unless you believe there's still time on the clock. And that kind of faith? It's exactly what's required in the spiritual life too.

Hebrews 11:1 (NLT) reminds us, "Faith shows the reality of what we hope for; it is the evidence of things we cannot see." You may not see a path forward—but if you have faith, you've got a foundation to move.

But faith alone isn't what makes a spiritual comeback possible—**grace** is. Ephesians 2:8 says, "God saved you by his grace when you believed. And you can't take credit for this; it is a gift from God." Grace is the reason you're never too far gone. Grace is what welcomes you back when you've run out of plays.

You don't need perfection—you need permission to start again. God isn't surprised you need a comeback. He's been waiting at the line of scrimmage, playbook in hand, whispering, "Let's run it again."

You don't need perfection—you need permission to start again. God isn't surprised you need a comeback. He's been waiting at the line of scrimmage, playbook in hand, whispering, "Let's run it again."

Comebacks Through Christ - Josh Hamilton's Story

Josh Hamilton had it all: talent, potential, a major league contract. But addiction nearly destroyed his career—and his life. Drugs, alcohol, and bad decisions left him suspended from baseball and broken in every way.

But Josh found something in rehab that baseball couldn't give him: **Jesus**. He surrendered. He rebuilt. And in one of the greatest personal comebacks in sports history, he returned to MLB, became an All-Star, won MVP, and publicly credited his turnaround to God.

His story isn't perfect. Recovery is messy. But grace doesn't require perfect—just repentance. Josh reminds us: *"It's a God thing."*

Personal Story - Wendy's Diagnosis

When the doctor said, "Stage IV Pancreatic Cancer," time stood still. My wife Wendy was the strongest person I knew. We had plans. We had family. And suddenly, the entire game changed.

I wanted to pray—but I couldn't. I was overwhelmed. Paralyzed. My mind raced with family, fear, and what-ifs. I believed in God, but I couldn't find the words. That's when I began to understand that real prayer isn't always strong—it's surrendered.

Over time, I whispered what I could. I asked others to carry us in prayer when I didn't have the strength. And God met us there.

Wendy didn't lose her battle. She won. Because the moment she took her last breath on earth, she took her next breath in Heaven—healed, whole, and with her Savior. That's a comeback greater than anything this world can offer.

It took me time to see that. For days I didn't pray at all. I felt like I had lost, like my prayers had been ignored. But in that silence, God spoke. And that whisper changed everything.

Death didn't win. Christ did. And through that, I saw a deeper truth—sometimes the greatest victory doesn't look like what we expected, but it's more complete than we ever imagined.

When You Don't Feel Like Praying

This is where real comebacks begin—not in bold declarations, but in whispered doubts. Not when the stadium's loud—but when your soul is silent.

There was a stretch after Wendy's passing when I didn't pray at all. I was numb. Bitter. I asked myself, "Why should I pray if it didn't change the outcome?" But one night, sitting alone on the back porch as the sun set over the hills of Pennsylvania, I heard it—not audibly, but deep in my spirit: **"She is healed. Your prayers WERE answered."**

The next morning, I prayed again. Not eloquently. Not confidently. But honestly. That was my real comeback.

So if you don't feel like praying, ask yourself why. Sit in the silence. Let God meet you there. Psalm 46:10 says, "Be still, and know that I am God."

Romans 8:26 reminds us that the Holy Spirit prays for us with groanings too deep for words. When you don't know what to say—just show up. The Spirit fills in the gaps.

Don't fake it. Just take the next step. That's how comeback prayers are born.

The Real MVP of Every Comeback

This is the moment the cameras zoom in. The clock ticks down. The crowd holds its breath. It's the bottom of the ninth with two outs and the bases loaded, boom a grand slam. A buzzer-beater three from the corner pocket. A 67-yard field goal sailing through the uprights as time expires. A 50-foot putt on the 18th green. A perfect strike in the 10th frame to win the game by one pin. The Hail Mary miracle.

We've all seen the highlight reels. The impossible victories. The comeback wins that leave you speechless. But none of those compare to the greatest comeback of all time.

Because in the comeback of your soul, **you're not the hero of the highlight—Jesus is.**

He didn't just come through in the clutch. He came through when we were down for the count—dead in our sin, defeated by guilt, and separated from God. And He didn't walk off the field with a trophy... He walked out of the tomb with victory in His hands.

Romans 5:8 (NLT) says, "But God showed his great love for us by sending Christ to die for us while we were still sinners." That's the play that changed everything.

You and I were on the losing team. No hope. No rally coming. But Jesus stepped in. Took our penalty. Paid our fine. And offered us a new jersey. A new position. A whole new life.

And He's not asking you to prove yourself. He's just asking you to trust Him.

67

Romans 10:9 says, "If you openly declare that Jesus is Lord and believe in your heart that God raised him from the dead, you will be saved." That's the comeback invitation.

Maybe you've been fighting through loss, addiction, doubt, or silence. But if you've never said yes to Jesus—this is your moment. The play clock is ticking, but the invitation still stands.
The comeback of your soul starts here.
Prayer isn't just how you get back in the game. It's how you meet the One who already won it for you.

Final Note

(*A soft beat rolls in... the field clears... and we return to the booth one last time.*)

Hal Michaels:
"Well folks, that's the story. A player who started on the bench... and finished with purpose."

Troy Roman:
"Not perfect. Not polished. But faithful. Showed up. Kept praying. Kept trusting. That's what it takes."

Hal:
"And just when they thought they couldn't pray another word, they found their strength wasn't in the prayer... but in the One who heard it."

Troy:
"Let's not forget—the greatest comeback ever wasn't in the

fourth quarter. It was three days after the cross."

"There once was a warrior who didn't fight with a sword, but with a whisper.

Who didn't win with power, but with persistence.

Who knelt more than He stood.

Who bled so others could breathe.

And we call Him Jesus."

8

Chapter 8: Sudden Death Overtime — The Power of Prayer and Fasting

The stadium lights blazed brighter than ever, cutting through the dark sky like swords. The regulation clock had run out—but the battle wasn't over.

The roar of the crowd was deafening. Tension wrapped around every player like a heavy fog. Every heartbeat, every breath, every movement from here on out mattered.

This was sudden death overtime.

Hal Michaels adjusted his headset and spoke with intensity into his mic.

"Folks, you can feel it—this isn't just another drive. This is legacy time. One play can make you a legend—or a memory."

Beside him, Troy Roman leaned forward, his voice low and electric.

"That's right, Hal. No margin for error now. It's fourth quarter faith multiplied. It's digging deeper than you ever thought you could."

As the team captains met at midfield, the referee stood tall, his whistle hanging at his lips. He looked each captain in the eye—and then, over the stadium speakers, his voice boomed.

"Gentlemen, welcome to sudden death overtime. Here are the rules: First one to cross the goal line wins. No timeouts. No second chances. Every play counts. Every decision matters. And remember this: In spiritual overtime, talent isn't enough. Hustle isn't enough. You need hunger. Real hunger. You clear the field. You cut the noise. You fight from your soul—not your strength. That's called fasting. And the ones who fast and pray? Those are the ones who win the battles that matter."

The captains shook hands. The coin flipped high into the night sky. The illusion that anything casual was left disappeared. This was for everything.

I've seen a lot of games end in overtime. But one moment from history sticks with me—one that, even though it broke my young Cowboys-loving heart, taught me a powerful lesson about what it means to fight for every inch.

It was the Ice Bowl. December 31, 1967. Cowboys versus Packers. Temperature: −13°F, with a brutal −48°F wind chill. Lambeau Field was a block of ice—even the heating system beneath the turf froze solid that day.

Fourth quarter. Final seconds. Packers at the one-yard line. Bart Starr, cold and battered, called his own number. On a quarterback sneak, behind a desperate surge from his linemen, he drove himself over the goal line to win the game.

That play wasn't about strength alone. It was about focus, heart, and absolute surrender to the mission. That's what fasting and prayer feel like in spiritual overtime.

You deny yourself. You strip away the noise. You lay it all down to move the ball across the line when nothing else will do.

Hal Michaels brought the focus back to the field.

"And speaking of legacy moments, Troy—let's head into

71

the film room and show how the greats handled overtime situations."

Troy Roman leaned into the broadcast.

"Absolutely, Hal. Let's roll the film."

First Drive: Jesus in the Wilderness

Troy Roman set the scene vividly.

"Picture it: Forty days of scorching sun, cold desert nights. Jesus—alone, exhausted, starving. Right when His flesh is at its lowest point, Satan launches the blitz."

"Then Jesus was led by the Spirit into the wilderness to be tempted there by the devil. For forty days and forty nights He fasted and became very hungry." (Matthew 4:1–2, NLT)

Troy's voice carried the weight of the moment.

"Jesus wasn't caught off guard. Fasting tuned His spirit. When Satan attacked, Jesus countered every lie with Scripture."

Result: Jesus left the wilderness undefeated, untouched, and victorious. Fasting didn't weaken Him—it armored Him.

Second Drive: Esther's Life-or-Death Stand

Troy continued, voice rising with urgency.

"Now shift to another high-stakes drive—Queen Esther. Alone in the pocket, the fate of her people on the line."

"Go and gather together all the Jews of Susa and fast for me. Do not eat or drink for three days, night or day. My maids and I will do the same. And then, though it is against the law, I will go in to see the king. If I must die, I must die." (Esther 4:16, NLT)

"Esther didn't rush in blind. She fasted first. She prepared her heart, not just her courage."

Result: The king's heart softened. The Jewish people were saved. Fasting carried her across the goal line.

Third Drive: The Early Church's First Big Draft

Troy's voice steadied for the next clip.
   "The early church needed clarity. No time for guessing—only for fasting."

"One day as these men were worshiping the Lord and fasting, the Holy Spirit said, 'Appoint Barnabas and Saul for the special work to which I have called them.'" (Acts 13:2, NLT)

"They heard clearly because they cleared the distractions."

Result: The greatest missionary movement in history was launched. Fasting led to clarity. Clarity led to action. Action led to world-shaking impact.

The cameras shifted back to the field.

Jesse Walker's Moment of Destiny

Hal Michaels raised his voice as the play unfolded.

"Here it is, folks—overtime, sudden death. Jesse Walker—the man who's been fasting all week, leaning on prayer, digging deeper than his body could go."

The ball snapped. Jesse sprinted toward the corner of the end zone. His legs burned. His lungs screamed.

Troy Roman jumped in.

"Quarterback launches it high—spiraling—Jesse goes up—one hand—TOUCHDOWN! He hauls it in, drags the toes—it's good!"

Hal's voice cracked with excitement.

"Victory, folks! Jesse Walker conquers sudden death overtime! That's fasting-fueled faith if I've ever seen it!"

And as the stadium erupted in celebration, it was clear:

It wasn't talent that won the day.

It wasn't strength.

It was trust—trust in the One who calls us to fight our battles first on our knees.

Coach Blaze's Fasting Tips for Rookies

Coach Blaze leaned against the whiteboard, arms crossed, voice firm but encouraging.

"Now listen—not everyone starts with a forty-day fast. That's varsity level. If you're just getting started, here's how you train:"

Fasting Drills for Rookies:

- Start with one meal. Skip breakfast or lunch and spend that time in prayer instead.
- Fast for a short window—six hours, twelve hours, whatever challenges you.
- Stay hydrated. Drink water.
- Focus your mind—fasting without prayer is just dieting.
- Ask God to speak clearly—even if the hunger gnaws a little.

"Training makes you stronger. Discipline stretches your spirit. Don't get legalistic—get intentional. Because when the real overtime comes, you'll be ready."

Prayer Drill: Your First Fast Challenge

- Pick one meal this week to fast.
- During that hour, find a quiet place and pray intentionally.
- Ask God for breakthrough, clarity, and renewed hunger for Him.

Coach Blaze Locker Room Talk

Coach Blaze stood before the team, voice fierce and full of fire.

"You don't win sudden death battles because you're the fastest or the flashiest. You win because you prepared in the quiet. You stripped away the noise. You tuned your heart to hear the Coach's voice."

He paced in front of the players, eyes locked in.

"Fasting isn't a magic trick. It's obedience. It's focus. It's surrender. Championships are won long before game day. Victories are sealed long before the clock starts."

He stopped, voice dropping to a sharp intensity.

"You fight your battles on your knees first. You fast to sharpen your hearing. You pray to strengthen your hands. You trust— not your legs, not your arms—but the One who already holds the victory."

Coach Blaze pointed toward the exit sign above the tunnel.

"And when your sudden death moment comes—don't just survive.

Win it.

Fast. Pray. Stand.

And watch the enemy fall."

Hal Michaels closed it out perfectly.

"And speaking of Jesse—let's head down to the field. Ellie An-drus is standing by with our MVP for the Postgame Interview."

Chapter 9: Postgame Interview with the Prayer Warrior

Hal Michaels (from the booth):

"Well folks, what a season it's been. We've seen highs, lows, comebacks, and quiet victories. And at the center of it all? Jesse Walker—a guy who started on the bench and found his footing through prayer."

Troy Roman:

"Yeah Hal, he's shown us what grit looks like—not in the weight room, but in the prayer room. And now, we're going to throw it down to the field where our very own Ellie Andrus is standing by for the postgame interview."

(*The field is chaos. Gatorade pours over the head of Jesse Walker. The crowd cheers. Cameras flash. Victory music swells in the background.*)

Ellie Andrus (smiling, dodging a towel):

"Well, I guess that answers the first question—this was a win. Jesse, congratulations. From benchwarmer to prayer warrior.

What's going through your heart right now?"

Jesse Walker:

"Honestly? Gatorade and Gratitude. And disbelief. I didn't think I had what it took. But God wasn't asking for perfect—He was asking me to show up."

Ellie:

"Let's go back. You started this season struggling to even make the prayer team. Midway through, it looked like the answers weren't coming. What changed?"

Jesse:

"It was after that blowout loss on the road to Philly. That was a long, quiet flight home. I didn't want to talk. Didn't want to pray. I just sat there staring out the window wondering if I even belonged on the team. And in the silence, God spoke. Not audibly—but in that deep-down place where only He can reach. He reminded me He wasn't asking for polished prayers—He just wanted me. That didn't change the outcome of the game, but it changed my heart. That was the turning point."

Ellie:

"There were a couple moments you almost gave up. We saw it from the booth. What pulled you through?"

Jesse:

"Honestly? Romans 8:26. *'And the Holy Spirit helps us in our weakness...'* That one line reminded me that even when I had nothing left to say, I wasn't praying alone."

Ellie:

"You trained hard—drills, playbook, film study. What part of the training really stuck with you?"

Jesse:

"Having a game plan. The weekly prayer layout changed everything. I didn't wander—I had purpose. And memorizing verses gave my prayers depth. It turned repetition into relationship. Joshua 1:8 reminds us to meditate on God's Word day and night. That became my playbook."

Ellie:

"There are players watching this who haven't left the bench yet. They think they're not good enough to pray. What would you say to them?"

Jesse:

"I'd tell them this: God's not grading your prayers. He's inviting you into the huddle. 1 Thessalonians 5:17 says *'Never stop praying.'* That's it. No fancy words. Just don't quit."

Ellie:

"Okay, last question—next season. What's your offseason plan?"

Jesse (grinning):

"Back to the gym. Not the physical one—the prayer one. More scripture, more journaling, more listening. Because prayer warriors aren't built in public. They're built in the quiet."

Ellie (laughing): "Well Jesse, before we wrap—looks like we've got some questions from the booth."

(Camera cuts to the booth where Hal, Troy, and Coach Blaze are waiting with smiles.)

Troy Roman: "I watched your footwork change midseason. Your rhythm. There had to be a verse or a practice that helped you settle in. What was it?"

Jesse: "Psalm 46:10—*'Be still and know that I am God.'* I stopped treating prayer like a performance. That verse slowed me down and gave me space to just be with God."

Coach Blaze (leaning in): "Alright, son. You know I'm big on drills and reps. What's the one spiritual habit you're taking with you into next season?"

Jesse: "Consistency. Even on the days I don't feel it. I'm showing up. Because I know the wins happen in the quiet places—when no one else is watching."

Ellie (grinning): "Well said. Gentlemen in the booth—final thoughts?"

Hal Michaels: "This was one for the books. We watched a benchwarmer become a warrior—and not because of talent, but because of trust."

Troy Roman: "Jesse reminded us that real change isn't flashy. It's built one quiet prayer at a time."

Coach Blaze: "And let this be a word to anyone still sitting it out: The only way to lose... is not to pray."

Coach Blaze (narrating): "As the crowd began to thin and the lights started to dim, Jesse made his way toward the tunnel. But before he stepped off the field, he paused. A man was waiting—quiet, steady, standing just beyond the shadows. No credentials. No team gear. Just a white towel slung over His shoulder... and eyes that had clearly seen every play."

"Jesse smiled, nodded, and whispered, 'Thank You, Coach.'"

"The Man in the tunnel gave a simple nod back and said, 'Well done.'"

"Later, as Jesse walked down the hallway toward the locker room, he passed the Wall. The one reserved for those who gave everything in the quiet, in the hidden moments—the Hall of Faith."

"Someone was already there, etching his name into the marble."

Jesse Walker – Warrior of the Whisper

'The prayers of the righteous produce great results.' – James 5:16

"Prayer season never ends. The ones who keep showing up in the quiet? Those are the ones who make the Hall."

A Letter from the Author

If you've made it this far, thank you. You've stuck with me through humor, honesty, and some pretty intense film study on what it means to pray.

This book isn't written by an expert. It's written by someone who got cut from the prayer team more than once. Who still forgets to pray. Who still fumbles his words. But who knows—without a doubt—that prayer is where the real work happens.

If you take one thing away from this journey, let it be this: **God isn't waiting for the perfect version of you to show up. He's waiting for the present version.** The one who's willing to whisper, "Lord, I need You."

So keep running the plays. Keep doing the drills. Keep showing up to the huddle. And when you don't know what to say, remember—your MVP already called the winning play.

See you on the field,

Raymond

10

Chapter 10: Your Offseason Training Plan: Mastering the ACTS Prayer Method

The final whistle may have blown, but true champions know that what happens between seasons matters just as much as what happens during the game.

Training doesn't stop when the lights go out.

Growth doesn't end when the crowd goes home.

And prayer doesn't end when the crisis passes.

Prayer warriors aren't made on the field.

They're made in the unseen hours—the offseason work that prepares them for the next battle.

Hal Michaels said it best from the booth: "The real work starts now."

And he's right.

This next season of your life—whatever God calls you into—will demand more prayer, more focus, more dependence on Him than ever before.

That's why today's final coaching session isn't a highlight reel.

It's a training plan.

And it starts with one of the simplest—and most powerful—prayer frameworks available:

The ACTS Prayer Method.

Troy Roman Breaks Down the Playbook

Troy Roman adjusted his headset and leaned into the mic with the energy of a coach who knew the importance of fundamentals.

"Fans, listen up.

Every great player, no matter how many touchdowns they score, still drills the basics.

Prayer is the same way.

The ACTS method isn't flashy.

But it's proven.

It's how you build a prayer life that wins long after the stadium clears out."

Troy flipped the first page of the Playbook and began the breakdown.

A – Adoration: Start With Worship

"You don't start a drive by demanding the ball.

You start by recognizing who's calling the plays.

Adoration is where you come before God and simply worship Him for who He is—His power, His goodness, His mercy.

It's about putting Him back on the throne of your heart where He belongs."

- Praise God's character.
- Declare His greatness, not just your needs.
- Focus your heart upward before you ever look inward or outward.

C – Confession: Clear the Field

"You can't run a clean route if the field's covered in junk.
Confession is how you clear the field.
Be honest about where you missed the block, fumbled the ball, or blew the assignment.
Don't hide. Don't spin it.
Own it."

- Acknowledge specific sins.
- Trust in God's forgiveness and cleansing (1 John 1:9).
- Get spiritually reset before moving forward.

T – Thanksgiving: Celebrate the Wins

"Gratitude keeps your heart hungry but humble.
Thanksgiving is where you thank God—not just for the big miracles, but for the small mercies too.
You celebrate every first down, every successful block, every open door He provided."

- Thank Him for answered prayers, even the ones you forgot you prayed.
- Thank Him for protection, provision, guidance, and grace.
- Thanksgiving fuels faith for the battles still ahead.

S – Supplication: Call the Play

"Now you ask.

Supplication is where you call the play at the line of scrimmage.

You tell God your needs—for yourself, for your team, for the mission He's given you.

You pray bold, specific, faith-filled prayers."

- Pray for personal needs, but don't stop there.
- Pray for others—your family, your church, your friends, your enemies.
- Pray for wisdom, courage, healing, revival.

Troy finished his breakdown and closed the Playbook.

"Simple. Clear. Proven.

When you pray ACTS, you're not just firing Hail Mary passes.

You're building a winning gameplan—one prayer at a time."

Coach Blaze Locker Room Talk

Coach Blaze stood before the team—no whistle, no clipboard, just fire in his voice.

"You want to be a prayer warrior?

You want to be the kind of believer Hell fears and Heaven applauds?

Then don't wait for a crisis to start training.

Start today.

Start small if you have to.

But start."

He pointed to the chalkboard behind him, where four simple

letters were written:

A – Adoration
C – Confession
T – Thanksgiving
S – Supplication

"This is your offseason training plan.

Master it.

Drill it.

Make it muscle memory.

Because the next time the enemy comes charging at you in overtime, you won't panic—you'll pray.

And you'll be ready."

Play of the Day Drill

Your Challenge:

- Take 10 minutes today.
- Walk through each step of ACTS—Adore, Confess, Thank, and Supplicate.
- Write your prayer out in a journal, or speak it aloud while walking, driving, or sitting quietly.

Repeat this drill every day this week.

Watch how your prayer life deepens, strengthens, and gains clarity.

Final Charge: From the Playbook to the Prayer Field

The season may be over.

But the battle isn't.

The best players train harder when no one's watching.

The best warriors pray deeper when no one's listening.

This is your offseason.

This is your training ground.

This is your moment to build the kind of prayer life that wins when it matters most.

The Prayer Playbook is in your hands now.

The field is yours.

Go run your race.

And pray like a champion.

Coach Blaze stepped back onto the field one last time. His voice wasn't loud — it didn't need to be. Every player leaned in, hanging on his words.

"Prayer Warriors aren't built in the spotlight.

They're built in the offseason.

When no one's cheering.

When no one's looking.

When you grind when others quit."

"So lace up. Show up. Pray hard. Train smart.

God's ready for champions — not spectators."

He paused, pointing toward the stands, almost as if he could already see the finish line far beyond the stadium lights.

"The ultimate championship isn't holding a trophy here.

It's hearing the King say, 'Well done, good and faithful servant.'

That's the victory that matters most."

Coach Blaze smiled and said,

"Now get to work. Training camp starts today."

Link to ACTS Prayer Worksheet: https://discipleblueprint.com/wp-content/uploads/2024/10/ACTS-Prayer-Method-Worksheet-1.pdf

11

A Prayer for the 'Boys

A Final Prayer (For the Dallas Cowboys)

Important Disclaimer:

This prayer is meant as a joke.
  Well, sort of.
  Mostly.

Lord,
  You tell us in Your Word that all things are possible through You.
  And Lord, I believe You. I really do.
  But if I'm honest, there's a part of me that's starting to wonder if that even applies to the Dallas Cowboys winning another Super Bowl.
  For decades now, we've prayed.
  We've hoped.
  We've endured winters colder than Lambeau Field without a

playoff win to warm our hearts.

We've watched miracle finishes happen for everyone else.

We've seen teams with no history and no tradition hoist the Lombardi Trophy.

And we're still... waiting.

Lord, we thank You for Jerry Jones for building the finest stadium money could build even if championships weren't included in the price of admission.

We thank You for his loyalty, his enthusiasm, and his willingness to spare no expense—except maybe when it comes to hiring a real General Manager.

But Lord, it's been **28 years** since we even *appeared* in a Super Bowl.

Twenty-eight.

The Israelites wandered the wilderness for forty years, but even they made it to the Promised Land eventually.

They may have complained about manna, but at least they didn't get blown out and embarrassed by the Packers in a playoff game on national TV.

Lord, we remember when the Dallas Cowboys were feared—

When **Bob Hayes** outran not just defenders but Olympic sprinters.

When **Bob Lilly** slammed Bob Griese into the turf so hard in the Super Bowl it echoed across the decades.

When **Roger Staubach** heaved a prayer into the sky and **Drew Pearson** pulled down the original Hail Mary.

When **Troy Aikman**, **Emmitt Smith**, and **Michael Irvin** turned January into an annual tradition of trophies and celebrations.

Those were the glory days, Lord.

We remember them.

We believe in miracles because we *lived through them once.*

Maybe—if it's not too much trouble—you could send a few angels down to Jerry's office.

Maybe one could whisper some wisdom.

Maybe another could gently, lovingly, whisper in his ear:

"You are not a great General Manager."

"If you worked for a team you didn't own, you would have been fired twenty years ago."

And Lord—if it's not too much to ask—

Could You maybe let **Coach Tom Landry** have a word with You?

He's already up there, fedora firmly in place, likely shaking his head every playoff weekend.

Maybe he could step into Your throne room and plead on behalf of us poor, tired, faithful fans who still bleed blue and silver even when it hurts.

Lord, if You still part Red Seas...

If You still rain manna from Heaven...

If You can raise dry bones to life...

Surely You can resurrect a championship team from the ashes in Dallas.

We know it would take a miracle.

We're fine with that.

After all, You're still in the miracle business.

And now, Lord—

We're in the prayer business.

In Christ's name I pray, Amen.

Appendix A: Welcome to the Team — Disciple Blueprint

Hal Michaels leaned back in his chair, smiling into the mic.

"Well folks, if you've enjoyed the game plan in this book, you're going to love what's next. Because training doesn't stop when the clock runs out."

Troy Roman nodded.

"That's right, Hal. Real champions never stop growing. And that's exactly why Coach here built Disciple Blueprint—an online training ground for prayer warriors, disciple-makers, and everyday believers who want to take their faith to the next level."

Coach Blaze stepped into frame, clipboard in hand.

"Disciple Blueprint isn't just a website. It's a community. A place for rookies, starters, and Hall of Famers alike to keep training, keep learning, and keep winning. Bible studies. Devotionals. Prayer tools. Strategy guides. Everything a growing Christian needs to stay game-ready."

Hal chuckled.

"Sounds like a team worth joining, Coach."

Coach Blaze grinned.

"Doors are always open. Check it out at www.discipleblueprint. com and join the roster. We'll see you in the locker room."

www.ingramcontent.com/pod-product-compliance
Lightning Source LLC
Chambersburg PA
CBHW051638120626
46551CB00014B/2119